The Making of a
MEAN GIRL
IN MINISTRY

EVANGELIST DR. TRACEY HOLLIS

ISBN: 978-1-965082-39-3

Publishing By:

The Acklin Group/ LERG EMPOWERMENT

www.lergempowermentusa.org

Editing/Design:

DemiCo National, LLC

www.DemiCoNational.com

Table of Content

Foreword

Ministry is a sacred calling that requires not only anointing but also integrity, humility, and a heart aligned with God's purpose. However, as Evangelist Dr. Tracey Hollis so powerfully unveils in *The Making of a Mean Girl in Ministry*, not all who enter this space operate from a place of love and righteousness. Too often, competition, jealousy, insecurity, and division creep into ministry, leaving behind wounds that were never meant to exist in the body of Christ. This book is a much-needed conversation that exposes these hidden struggles and calls for a higher standard among women in ministry.

From the very first page, Dr. Hollis challenges readers to take a deep look at their hearts and intentions. Are we truly walking in our divine calling, or are we seeking validation from people instead of God? Have we uplifted our sisters in Christ, or have we fallen into the trap of gossip, comparison, and silent rivalry? These are difficult but necessary questions, and this book does not shy away from them. Instead, it provides clarity, wisdom, and biblical truths that encourage healing and realignment with God's will.

As I read this book, I found myself reflecting on the power of true sisterhood in ministry. It is not about titles, platforms, or self-promotion; it is about serving with a pure heart, edifying others, and standing united in faith. Dr. Hollis reminds us that ministry should never be a battlefield of egos but a mission field for souls. If we are to be effective, we must first heal from the traumas that make us guarded, competitive, and, at times, unkind. True anointing is never threatened by another's success; it thrives in unity, grace, and obedience to God.

To every woman who has ever felt the sting of rejection, the pain of betrayal, or the pressure to prove herself in ministry, this book is for you. It is a call to transformation—a charge to operate in love, integrity, and spiritual maturity. As you all turn these pages, I encourage you to embrace the wisdom within, allowing it to refine and shape you into the woman God has called you to be. May this book challenge you, empower you, and lead you into a renewed season of growth, accountability, and divine purpose.

—Dr. Cynthia Whaley

Chapter 1:

What One Won't Do, Another One Will

Have you ever heard the subliminal statement, *"What one won't do, another one will"*? In some instances, this statement may be true. It all depends on the narrative. I have witnessed this on many occasions. When you are on a God-divine assignment, be sure that those who are connected to you are on the same mission. When God delivers a prophetic message, it is up to us to be in protective mode of the anointing; to excavate.

As we matriculate through life, you will experience individuals with hidden agendas that aren't conducive to us. It is gut-wrenching and disappointing. This is exactly how God feels when we are slothful and disobedient. The Bible says, in **1 Samuel 15:22,** that it is better to be obedient than to sacrifice. The definition of obedience is compliance with an order, request, or law; submission to another's authority. Like, duh? God is testing our faith, trust, loyalty, and truths.

While excavating, I was reminded of a strong and mighty vessel named Samson. He was anointed and appointed by God. His gifts and talents were orchestrated by God. His gift was strength, but his calling was to judge. He was mandated from the beginning to obey protocol, laws, and principles. This mantle that Samson possessed could have been chosen for another. Yes; the gifts and callings are without repentance, but God qualifies us to obey. Our purpose has specific instructions, directions, and paths that must be taken into consequential consideration. Either we will comply or be marked by impropriety.

Oftentimes, individuals who are called and chosen seem to test their limits with God. It's me.

I've done this. We are like children, given an inch and taking a mile. Samson was mandated to follow the principles, laws, and the Spirit of God. He was consecrated by going through a Nazirite vow, which explained the dos and don'ts. He must not touch the dead, drink wine, marry outside of his faith, or dishonor his parents, and no, never cut his hair. But of course, he challenged protocol.

He was on a self-rising campaign to do what was pleasing to himself. He ignored the prompting of God's Spirit. He only obeyed his lustful and self-righteous nature. We've all been there. Haven't we?

Pride is stated to be a violation against God. The Bible declares that pride comes before a downfall. When God's grace and mercy become insufficient, we will be marked with substantial consequences. We may pay with our lives, afflictions, loss, grief, termination, misfortunes, curses, cycles, a reprobate mind, or self-inflicted sabotage.

It would be wise to ask God: *What are your requirements for my specific purpose and destiny?*

Everyone's calling wasn't created the same. What one person may get away with, another will suffer tremendously for. Rebellion is revealed in **1 Samuel 15:23**. It says that rebellion is the sin of witchcraft, meaning in God's eyes, we are actively resisting or defying authority. This is considered a practice of witchcraft. Woah! In other words, when we do anything to please ourselves, we are considered untrustworthy individuals.

God also anointed and appointed Saul as king with the help of the prophet Samuel. King Saul's assignment was to carry out the annihilation of the evil Amalekites. He was instructed to kill all males, females, children, nursing babies, flocks, and crops. God also warned him not to take spoils from a cursed territory. Those were solid instructions.

Of course, he did not fully follow the protocol. He kept King Agag and his unnoticeable pregnant wife alive. Saul brought shame and displeasure to God and to Israel. God, who is declared the Alpha (the Beginning) and the Omega (the Ending), was not pleased. The nerve and audacity of Saul! God was sick and tired of his shenanigans, pride, arrogance, and supreme disobedience. God literally fired him. Yet Saul still had to conduct business as usual, even in his termination. My God!

How can God trust us to complete a painstaking task? This is where our character is examined. Are we truly for God? These are questions we must consciously ask ourselves daily: *Am I pleasing God properly?* He will not be mocked.

You are safer in 5 p.m. traffic than playing with Abba. God is multifaceted and will make the necessary shift for the betterment of society. You will be demoted, and another will be promoted. The new one will have a pure heart, clean hands, good intentions, and an understanding of what is required. She will take the laws, protocols, vows, and covenants seriously.

Do not find yourself as an outcast to God. If you do, it will breed jealousy, envy, strife, contention, resentment, suspicion, and sabotage. Do not be like Samson or Saul. Both were tormented, tortured, and death was their portion. Yes, Samson repented and asked for one last request. God granted him the strength to obliterate his adversaries, including Delilah, the prohibited wife.

As women in ministry, it is vitally imperative to comply with the laws, instructions, and directions from God. Be sure that we are prepared to carry out the moves of God. Be sure that the oath we took is upheld to a high standard. Be aware that our *yes* is insured. *Lord, wherever You send me, I will go.* Remain vigilant and humble. Stay in your own designated lane. Do not resort to crash-out behavior.

Friendly Reminder #1:

Complete the assignment unhindered. Be sure that God called you to this. If not, you will be fired. He will raise another in your presence. And this one? She'll be more attractive, anointed, intelligent, creative, obedient, peaceful, a trailblazer, a fire-starter, and *that girl*!

Friendly Reminder #2:

Don't be punished for your own choice. Samson and King Saul had a choice. They chose to disobey God. Both were fired and brought to open shame. Do not be like them, girlies. Disobedience will cost you the peace and happiness in your life. Receive the blessings, not the curses.

Chapter 2:

Recruitment vs. Anointed

As we know, it is better to allow the anointing on your life to draw than to recruit. The term *recruit* means to enlist, essentially, to persuade someone to join, follow, or become a member. The term *anointed* means to choose someone or something for a particular purpose. In other words, you were anointed and appointed for a specific task.

In the book of Esther, I came to the conclusion that Haman, an Agagite, prime minister, and royal vizier to King Xerxes, was a descendant of King Agag. King Agag was killed and cut to pieces by the prophet Samuel, something King Saul was supposed to do. Haman was on a recruitment and revenge mission to completely annihilate the Jews, God's chosen destinies. With his position and closeness to King Xerxes, Haman gained access and influence to carry out his own will.

In this era, we've experienced individuals using their influence and affluence to cause division in society. Haman's hatred ran so deep that he wanted to avenge his bloodline. Remember, we are born into sin and shaped in iniquity. Due to the nature of King Agag's assassination, the queen (his wife) was secretly angry. King Saul had allowed her life, and she birthed hatred into the earth. Haman was marked from birth. His bloodline represented an incomplete violation against God.

We must examine the full picture. Haman was filled with pride, resentment, hatred, jealousy, envy, strife, rage, murder, and violence. Likewise, we must examine our own character in ministry.

Some individuals hold titles, positions, degrees, and honors, but lack character, integrity, loyalty, and individuality. Do not allow the spirits of pride, arrogance, and generational curses to get you evil-marked. The Bible says that the gifts and callings are without repentance, meaning, God predestined you and will not take His gifts back.

Oftentimes, I've witnessed individuals recruit people who are mentally and emotionally vulnerable. Their intentions are impure. They intentionally pervert others, turning them against you. Your confidence, God-fidence, wit, intelligence, obedience, and anointing make them insecure.

When we stay in the lane God has set before us, we should not monitor what our sister in Christ is doing. Your calling, from the womb, made you a target. Hell was terrified when your name was announced in Heaven. Your life has a standard, and you will not compromise for popularity. They may operate in charisma, but they lack the anointing to break yokes, bondages, ungodly ties, diseases, afflictions, and curses.

Haman recruited his wife and ten sons to go against God's destinies. God allowed His people to fall temporarily into the hands of their adversaries, but only to execute divine justice. Mordecai, appointed by King Xerxes as a gatekeeper at the king's gate in Susa, stayed alert with keen vision and sharp hearing. Anything suspicious, he reported to the king. Because of his integrity and loyalty, Mordecai was quickly and honorably promoted. His new title? Grand Vizier.

This was the ram in the bush, now working closely with the opposition.

Side Note: God's name is never mentioned in the book of Esther. That's because God didn't need an introduction. He is the Alpha and the Omega.

The most eloquent ram in the story was Esther. She was anointed and appointed for the position. Her beauty, essence, wit, intelligence, and good character made her *The One.* She was predestined for an assignment, not just to be queen, but to take on a suicide mission to save a generation of people.

When you are chosen, expect to become a target. The enemy will try to destroy your character, ministry, divine relationships, partnerships, collaborations, and businesses. It is extremely important to know who you are **and *Whose* you are**. Esther was prompted by Mordecai to speak up about what was going on in the kingdom. He sent word that Haman was plotting against the Jews and needed her influence as queen to intervene with her husband, King Xerxes.

At first, she didn't see Mordecai's request as life-threatening. She forgot who she really was, a Jew in a Persian kingdom. Mordecai, her cousin, reminded her that this assignment must be carried with care and urgency. Don't think for one second, he said, that your life and kingdom will be spared.

This is a reminder to us: **Never forget who you really are.** Don't get immersed in titles, positions, promotions, or accolades. We need strong mentors to hold us accountable.

With this realization, it was time to fast and pray, without food and water. Sometimes, we must refocus when the assignment could make or break us. Esther accepted this weighty task with a courageous mindset: *If I perish, then I perish.* That is the mindset of God's anointed Girlies.

Do not despise the severity of the assignment, because God owes you **currency.** This currency will follow you into your next level, into your future, and trickle down to your children's children. Each assignment comes with a burden, opposition, warfare, and sometimes, even death.

Esther put fear behind her and walked in faith. She invited herself into a room she wasn't invited to. She pushed past the naysayers and haters and asked for grace and peace. Her husband, King Xerxes, extended his scepter, a sign of peace. Her request was made known to the king, which agitated Haman. He hated Queen Esther because he couldn't understand who she really was. It was deeper than her being a woman or a queen, **she had the oil.** Just like you and I, Girlies.

The mean girls don't quite understand this oil. It keeps them up at night, monitoring your every move.

Luke 6:31 says, *"Do unto others as you would have them do unto you."* This is the law of reciprocity. Be wise about whom you conspire against. The Bible says in Psalm 105:15, *"Touch not my anointed, and do my prophets no harm."* That is the law of God.

You are better off playing in traffic than going against the great and terrible God. Haman found himself in a pickle. The gallows he had set up as a weapon of destruction soon became his own trap. King Xerxes ordered that Haman, his wife, and all ten of his sons be hanged.

Warning: Be careful who you plot evil against.

Devastation will meet you on that same ground.

Do not be the mean girl who pays the price. God's wrath has no limitations, and no expiration date. You reap what you sow.

Death, missed opportunities, illnesses, diseases, cancer, misfortunes, **these will be your payment.**

Friendly Reminder #3:

Recruiters' agendas are to separate, not unite.
Anointed Girlies have pure hearts, and they draw without effort.

Chapter 3:

The Monitoring and Covet Spirits

(Psycho Sisters)

These two spirits have very familiar traits: they want what you have and want to be you. Covet means to have a strong desire for something, especially something that belongs to someone else. This spirit's agenda is to become so obsessed that it seeks to destroy your mental, emotional, financial, and spiritual health, as well as your influence and affluence. That's why it is vitally important to have discernment and to follow up with wisdom.

The Bible says in **Proverbs 4:7**, *"Wisdom is the principal thing; therefore, get wisdom: and with all thy getting, get understanding."* This is an essential principle for anyone in ministry. As a Girlie in ministry, I recommend this tool, it will save your life, reputation, finances, and spirituality. Keep wisdom near and dear to your heart like a tablet. Monitoring means to observe and check the progress or quality of something over a period of time. This spirit wants to keep you under systematic review. The spirit's agenda is to put you under 24/7 surveillance, paying close attention to what you post on social media, what you wear to events, who you're connected to, what businesses you've launched, what books you've written, and even who you're dating.

For the anointed Girlies, these spirits operate with the intent to control. These are mean girl spirits, two of the most dangerous spirits that can cause sabotage if you're not careful. The oil you possess is weighty. In **Jeremiah 1:5**, God says, *"Before I formed you in the womb I knew you; before you were born I sanctified you; I ordained you a prophet to the nations."* Hello, Girlie, you're carrying nations. That's why people are so drawn to you. And that's why the mean Girlies don't understand.

I'm not saying that some mean girls aren't anointed, but they often lack the qualities of true godliness: confidence, altruism, competence, humility, innovation, wisdom, and perseverance. You will never need to emulate, imitate, or duplicate. God created you top-tier. When a mean girl isn't walking in her full potential, she tends to despise those who are. That's why it's so important to ask God what *your* purpose is and how to navigate *your* assignment.

God gave each of us our own lanes and races to run. Everyone has a process, and it's forged in fire. You will be tested through opposition, warfare, loneliness, and betrayal. Your oil and anointing cost something. I don't know what price you paid for your oil. I can only speak to mine. The warfare, trials, tribulation, and abandonment I've experienced would have had some people labeled as deranged. You don't know the cost of the oil in my life.

We have seasoned Mean Girls in ministry who find other like-minded individuals to manipulate. They do not have their own minds, nor do they seek confirmation from the Holy Spirit. These congregated spirits will be dismantled by the command of the armies of Heaven. Each evil gathering will be cursed in the name of Jesus. They will begin to turn on each other like snakes. God is going to disrupt and send confusion into their communication. The Bible says no weapon formed against us shall prosper, and every tongue that rises against us will be condemned. That is a promise. Decree and declare that the spirits' influence will become weak and a non-factor.

The Holy Spirit has a watchful eye on evil. The Lord will keep a divine hedge of protection over everything that you possess, your money, social media outlets, ministries, health, wealth, soul, land, mindset, house, career, marriage, children, promotions, elevation, collaborations, and divine doors will not fail. These spirits will lose their sense of smell and location in the spiritual realm. Do not think for one second to engage in a friendly quarrel. You do not owe these spirits anything but to annihilate them from your life.

As a Girlie in ministry, put on your big girl pants and strap up your combat boots, because we are prepared for war. Our mission is to ask the Holy Spirit to reveal individuals' intentions, hearts, and why they want to connect. Every connection is not ordained by God. We attracted them because of the oil, or they are waiting for the right appointed time to destroy your character. Some of my Girlies in ministry have become victims of mentee betrayal. **Daniel 6:6–24** is a great chapter to read. I recommend it for wisdom aesthetics. Daniel was a prophet ordained by

God. He was an obedient and honorable man. Remember, when you are in your designated niche, you will not be well-liked.

There was an agenda to plot against Daniel because of the favor on his life. Favor is not fair. Daniel was a man made by God, and he knew law and protocol. The three monitoring spirits that overtook the three men did not know who they were really against. Three unwise men went to the leader, King Darius, to secretly conspire a decree that would not allow anyone to pray to their God for the next 30 days.

King Darius, like most leaders, did not investigate the information before forming an opinion. Daniel was an intercessor who prayed consistently three times a day. No matter what the decree was, Daniel knew he was to worship and pray to God. Sometimes, that will come with a price. This decree was irrevocable.

King Darius realized too late that he had been deceived. The ones closest to you may often be the ones who sabotage you. Daniel had to be sent to the lions' den as a form of punishment. One thing I know about God, when you are in the right, He shall vindicate you. While the unwise men thought their plan had prevailed, King Darius was praying to Daniel's God.

Friendly Reminder #4:

God will have a ram in the bush just for you. That is why it pays to be obedient to God and not man.

Leaders, do not be deceived. Gain wisdom. Daniel was in the lions' den, but he was never touched. The angel of the Lord shut the mouths of the lions. Girlies, see, He will shut your enemies' and frenemies' mouths. You will be untouchable.

The same one that has conspired against you will fall to shame. The punishment will be reversed. Mean Girls, be wise in whom you seek to destroy. The same evil agendas you have for an individual will be the same irrevocable punishment you shall receive. Everything connected to you will suffer, your children, business deals, health, wealth, ministry, family, marriage, and influence will be affected.

Repent and turn quickly away from sin. Do not allow these two spirits to cause you to miss out on great connections and collaborations, new doors and relationships, sonships, partnerships, and promotions. Mean Girls, you have been warned. The Bible says in **Hebrews 2:1**, *"That warning comes before destruction."* That is not a threat, but a certified promise. Be delivered, set free, and made whole. There is a greater and positive purpose for you.

Chapter 4:

The Enemy Of Your Inner Me

There is an enemy on the inside of you that desires to keep you in captivity. Our responsibility as Girlies in ministry is to square up and go toe to toe with the enemy. Oftentimes, these enemies come through the bloodline, from our parents, grandparents, and so forth. These enemies show up as negative word curses, illiteracy, disobedience, complacency, and environmental challenges. You have the responsibility to change what is hindering you.

My challenges started while I was in my mother's womb. She was 14 years old and constantly lived in fear. My mother and father rejected me from birth. This spiritual force followed me for years. It also bred low self-esteem and anxiety, a great need for validation, and a deep sense of abandonment. This enemy had me under 24/7 surveillance, monitoring my every move.

At the age of 17, I encountered fornication. I was manipulated by my then-boyfriend. I wanted to abstain from sex, but I knew he would get it from another girl. I allowed the enemies of rejection and abandonment to hinder my good judgment. I never dealt with those spirits. I tried to sweep them aside, hoping things would get better.

As Girlies in ministry, I urge you to be honest with yourself and find a resolution to obliterate those inner enemies. It is not safe for you, or anyone, to be preaching and teaching without having successfully dealt with your issues. You can be anointed and appointed and still have unresolved struggles. We've read many stories about past and present icons who succumbed to their inner enemies. Be responsible enough to identify the actual root of the problem. It is not your family's responsibility; it is yours.

In the book of **Isaiah 37:31**, *the imagery of a tree taking root deep in the ground before bearing fruit above* signifies the importance of establishing a strong foundation before producing positive results. The agenda of the inner enemies is to cause chaos, "crash-outs," burnout, unhealed wounds, and to make you out to be a fool. Mean Girls, it is time to heal the little girl within. It is not recommended that you hide behind the pulpit, revivals, conferences, or other outlets. Sis, it's time to call yourself out.

Committing adultery while shading others from the pulpit is hypocrisy. You have never been held accountable to that inner enemy. Seriously, take a sabbatical and go to therapy. Whatever you are consistently struggling with, there are people in position to assist you. It's time to put an end to your deflection of the real problem.

Think about it. In the book of **Mark 5:25–34**, *there was a certain woman who had suffered with an issue of blood for twelve years*. The difference is, she acknowledged the issue and was desperately seeking help. She went to many physicians, but no regimen helped. I can only imagine what she was going through. She heard of a man named Jesus who was approaching her city. When you set your mind on things above and not beneath, be ready for the backlash. Since her condition was deemed unclean, she had to be isolated.

Girl Code Tip: Go into isolation until the perfect timing. Get refocused in your isolation season. Get quiet in your isolation season. Remain committed to the process.

Anywho, individuals in the city were discouraging the unknown woman. My question is: why didn't they encourage her to see Jesus, the man who raised the dead, healed the sick, the blind, the diseased, and the lame? You know why? They enjoyed seeing her suffer. That is why it is important to advocate for yourself and set a standard.

When she went higher to see Jesus, the crowd pulled her back. She decided, *"I will not miss this opportunity to encounter Jesus."* If I can just touch the hem of Him, then I will be made whole. That was pure determination. You go, Girlie. She went into a low position and stretched until the mission was complete. She touched the hem of Him, and immediately the blood ceased. You see, the enemy that plagued her for years finally left.

Hey, Mean Girl. Be determined to go on a mission to cease and desist every inner enemy that wants you to succumb to it. In the book of **Proverbs 18:21,** Solomon says**,** *"Death and life are in the power of the tongue, and those who love it will eat its fruit."* It's time to be held accountable. Be delivered from issues of rape, molestation, abandonment, jealousy, strife, contention, resentment, lying, unforgiveness, low self-esteem, low self-worth, cheating, alcoholism, promiscuity, adultery, leprosy, drama, mommy issues, daddy issues, perversion, lust, rejection, identity crisis, stubbornness, validation-seeking, tempers, clapbacks, imitation, fraudulence, misfortune, impoverished mindsets, dependency, procrastination, family traumas, bad behaviors, and so forth.

Your reputation depends on it.

Mean Girl, if you have caused discord among your Girlies in ministry, it is time to ask for forgiveness. Make it right in the eyesight of God and the individual. If you strive for peace, it will find you. Mean Girl, strive for healing, and it will find you. Do not allow those issues to control you any longer. Once you have been delivered, maintain your deliverance. Go forth and be free to be welcomed back into the Girlies in ministry.

Chapter 5:

Paid The Price Vs Paid For It

Many of the afflictions come upon the righteous, but the Lord delivers them all. This tells me there is hope in suffering. Affliction means a state of pain, distress, grief, or misery. Hannah was very familiar with difficult times. As an anointed individual, you will suffer for the sake of ministry.

Some **Girlies** that are in ministry have experienced different forms of cancer, divorce, the loss of a child, mental breakdowns, and much more. You will be tried and tested in the fire. Some afflictions will almost take you out, but I can guarantee, it is the mantle that must be birthed. I know it seems strange, but God knows the plans He has for you. God will pay you back in mantles, promotions, elevation, and financial currency.

Some promotions are the gift of healing, while others are to empower people not to give up. Not everyone is called to the **Fivefold** ministry. The **Fivefold** gifts are Apostle, Prophet, Evangelist, Pastor, and Teacher. Some are called to other auxiliaries in ministry, which are equally needed to push the vision. It is vitally imperative to know what your calling is. I advise you not to operate in error or in an illegal realm.

Being called to the **Fivefold**, I recommend that you choose a mentor whose goal is to hold you to a standard of excellence, accountability, teaching, and to help you accelerate to your next level. In this day and era, people are operating illegally, and it shows. This is not about popularity but about maturing what God has placed in your life. **In 2 Peter 1:10,** *Peter says, "make sure your calling and election is sure."* Over time, individuals have been exposed for purchasing a variety of *titles.*

It wasn't about igniting the people, but about gaining a sense of popularity and control. Self-exalted titles were built off financial wealth, mutilated fellowships, organizations, and gatekeeping cliques. God is not pleased with that type of behavior. Where is the integrity? Money will talk in doors, cliques, platforms, titles, and pulpits, but where does the anointing fit? How is it that you were called a prophet, but you can't prophesy a tick out of fur? How is it that you were called an evangelist, but you're gathering the people into leprosy and drama? How is it that you were called as an apostle, but you can't effectively pay your rent on a solid foundation? How is it that you were called as a teacher, but your own children don't know the first five books of the Bible? How is it that you were called as a pastor, but you are sleeping around with your member?

Those are questions that need to be answered.

It is time to set the record straight and be held accountable. Many individuals do not take these responsibilities seriously because their positions were bought, with Zelle, PayPal, Cash App, cash, credit card, or they slept their way into an opportunity. Like why? *Smh.* People are no longer waiting for God's perfect timing to make room for them. This is a microwave generation.

In the book of **Amos 1:7**, *it says that God's timing is perfect.* Before being ordained as an Evangelist, I was a minister in training for 6 years and a minister for 2 years. Absolutely nothing was handed to me. I completed training, courses, counseling sessions, and served the woman of God. My leader had to witness my willingness to change my life and what had me in a chokehold. My leader is my mother. She did not care that I was her daughter. Her position in ministry was to make sure that I was ready for this position.

I went through so much, but I never gave up. I made a decision to stop cursing, fighting, clapping back, fornicating, and clubbing. My calling was always in operation, but not at the standard of God. I had to come from among things that would cause a stain to my name and ministry. The making of Evangelist Dr. Tracey has been worth it.

As a Girlie in ministry, I've long suffered tremendously. God placed me on a probationary period to observe me carefully. I was put in a situation that could have potentially ended my career as an educator before becoming a school teacher. A student lied about me discussing a national case about a young Black male. I did not know all the details about the case.

I redirected each student to get back on track and discuss the assignment the teacher had left. The white male student went home and completely made false accusations against me. The principal told the teacher that he would conduct his own investigation. The teacher overreached his authority and confronted me. Two weeks prior, I made a vow to God that I was going to stop cursing.

I realized after this situation that this was God's doing. She snapped on me in front of five white male district employees. They got their trays and left. I saw one shaking his head in shame. While she was yelling at me, I saw the color green.

God allowed, in that very moment, for me to make a life-changing choice. I saw a panoramic view of me grabbing her by the neck and forcefully pushing her through the narrow glass window. I heard, in my ear, sirens and screams. I saw blood everywhere. It was a literal horror scene.

I did not want to disappoint God, myself, or my mother. We worked in the same school and district. After the prophetic premonition, the choice was in my hands. Instead, I did not allude to an argument. I was furious. I went into the clean lounge restroom, used all 500 sheets of paper towels, and got on my knees to worship God. I was thanking Him for self-control and for allowing me to be tested in the fire. Of course, I came out victorious.

The principal apologized, and she was written up. The blessings overtook me that semester. Oh yeah, I forgot to mention that I was a substitute teacher that year. God mantled me with favor and high esteem in His sight and man. I birthed a step and stroll team and was blessed to take over a teacher's class who was terminated. The sabotage spirit's agenda was to make God out to be a mockery and to taint my good name. I took account of the 9 fruits of the Spirit.

How do you call yourself a Prophetess but your tongue is a live wire ready to destroy a gathering? Your ministry will not be taken seriously and possibly marked. These are processes that we must endure before the elevation. How will you handle them? Elevation comes with a price and are you ready to pay?

I am reminded of the story in the Bible about Shadrach, Meshach, and Abednego; obedience before elevation. The Hebrew boys were tested by being obedient to God's law and forsaking worshipping other gods. The punishment was death. They were bound and thrown into the fiery furnace. The question is, how bad do you want it?

After King Nebuchadnezzar realized that the hand of God was upon them, he quickly promoted them. They paid the price for obedience. They were literally in the fire but came out smokeless. **Girlies**, be sure that your calling and election is sure. There is no need to throw shade from a tree that bears no fruit. This is not in regards to money. It has everything to do with whether God trusts you. Do you display self-control? I was not going to apply a mean girl spirit to sabotage my blessings. I maintained my deliverance while forging in the fire. No more mean girl cursing and old behavior patterns.

Friendly reminder #5:

Be intentional to maintain your deliverance, self-control, joy, peace, etc. Pray, fast, and seek wise counsel. It is time to be delivered, set free, and made whole from generational cycles, chains, bondages, and mind ties. Anointed Girlies paid the price, and the mean girls paid for it. Big difference!

Chapter 6:

Is This A Divine Connection Or A Sneaky Link

Ask yourself, is this a divine connection or a sneaky link? What do you mean by that? Are you sneaking and linking around to recruit certain individuals who do not like certain anointed Girlies in ministry? If so, you are a mean girl with unhealed traits. This is the time to be authentic with yourself and seek therapy from a licensed therapist, not your pastor.

In this day and era, enough is enough. You are too old to still conduct yourself as if you are worldly. It is time to take accountability and responsibility for your actions. We are considered the church, which means it is on the inside of us. Your church is plagued, wrinkled, and stained.

The Bible says in **Ephesians 5:27**, *"so that he (Jesus Christ) might present the church (us) to himself in splendor, without a spot or wrinkle, or any such thing, that she (us) be holy and without blemish."* These are not my words but the words from God. Take the moment for self-reflection. We have a plethora of worldly encounters to be pessimistic about. Girl, be cured from this ugly disease.

This is your call to be mended, improved, recuperated, convalesced, rehabilitated, and regenerated. The Bible says in **Psalms 55:22**, *"Cast your burdens on the Lord, and He will sustain you; He will* *never permit the righteous (you) to be moved."* In other words, it is necessary. Many new believers in Christ are departing from the edifice because we have elevated too many prima donnas and not enough venerated Girlies in Christ. When you begin to lose sight of the importance of igniting, impacting, empowering, and camaraderie, you've now ventured into territories of self-exaltation.

As King Nebuchadnezzar, who was anointed and appointed as ruler, he began to disregard God and worshipped himself. Those who were around him did not hold him accountable due to fear. We see this every day. He, like most people, ignored the Spirit of God. Warnings come before destruction.

His self-righteousness drove him to exile for seven years. He lost his mind. He made up his mind that it was about him and not the will of God. We've all been there more than once. As a mean girl trait, it is all about you, and you do not care who is affected.

He began to take on traits like the beasts of the field. After seven long years of self-infliction, of anger, disrespect, dishonor, and not being humble, he finally broke down. He said, "Yes, Lord." He immediately repented, and God restored him to the throne. God is faithful in trial and error.

God is searching for us to be obedient and to display humility. It is not all about us. It does not matter if you are called as a prophet, you will have to follow guidelines, laws, covenants, and mandates. Your character needs a purge. It is time for impeccable work.

The Bible says in **Psalms 51:7**, *"Cleanse me... and I shall be whiter than snow"*, meaning asking God to cleanse you of all your sins, transgressions, and iniquities. It is good when God chastises you because He really cares about you, not the title. Take a sabbatical for a season to be restored. Your restoration will be of a more ameliorated mindset. No more causing new girls in ministry to leave the church or groups.

We will not allow you to sow discord amongst us. You will be held totally accountable. Mean girl, you have a choice to do away with being an antagonist. Let us put an end to this matter. We, the Girlies in the Ministry, vow to uphold what is good and reject what is wrong.

We will build our character to a standard. The Bible says in **2 Corinthians 6:17**, *"Come out from them and be separate," says the Lord.* That concludes to no more accepting honors, invitations, outings, and engagements. This is not a divine connection but a sneaky link of pure corruption of good character.

Divine connections bring hope, future opportunities, new doors, endeavors, entitlements, mentorship, accountability, responsibility, wisdom, discernment, push, goals, peace, faith, and insight in ministry. These connections will encourage you to shift, and no longer will you desire the old.

We, the Girlies in Ministry, concur that we will not lose hope or vision while trusting in God. We will stand in solidarity with our Girlies in Christ. Let's grow an infectious positivity movement in Christ. We are renouncing and denouncing diabolic mindsets that are reclusive. Enough is enough. We, the Girlies in Ministry, summon all mean girls in ministry to do the right thing and become a new girl. It is in you. You got this! We will restore after you've gone through spiritual rehabilitation. We need you.

Final Notice:

You Have Been Warned

This warning applies to any woman in ministry who has caused discord, perjury, mental, emotional, financial, spiritual abuse, and disorderly conduct while working in the Five-Fold. It is time to stop deflecting your issues while preaching and teaching. The pulpit is not designed for a shade and clapback session, but was created to give biblical principles, truths, restoration, and to turn people away from sin. I charge you to be healed, delivered, set free, and made whole. Repent to God and to those that you hurt.

Turn away from your wicked and unhealed ways. Forgive as God has forgiven you. Speak good and not evil about your sisters in Christ. Be at peace within yourself. Do not allow your childhood traumas, diabolic drama, economic status, impoverished mindset, fornication, lies, disobedience, disbelief, demonic entanglements, demonic anchors, parental issues, sibling issues, jealousy, contention, self-inflicted behaviors, and sinful choices to keep you bound.

No longer use your prophetic gifts as a weapon of evil to keep others bound. Repent this day. Be free today and forevermore. No more congregating with other unhealed, like-minded women in ministry. Do not allow anyone to lay hands on you or speak into your eye gates while you are seeking God.

Come from among them. Those who do not have control of their own personal lives will control you without your knowledge and permission. Your first ministry is at home. Set the tone with your spouse, children, and so forth. It's time for you to advocate for your transformation and renewed life.

Let the blood of Jesus wash you clean as snow. Jesus came to reclaim you as His own. Ask Jesus to heal your heart. I know you've taken illegal assignments and positions, but release yourself today. If you comply with these terms, your reputation will be made new.

God desires you to apply **1 John 1:9**, **Revelation 3:8**, **Revelation 21:5-7**, and **Luke 5:32** to your life. God only desires you to replace the old character to be made new. Renew your mindset. Revive what He declared from your mother's womb. Rededicate your life, heart, mind, and purpose back to Him. He cares about you so dearly. Return with good morals and character, a new mindset, ministry ethics, and purpose-driven assignments from God. You Got This!

A Letter To My Anointed Girlies

Hi to my anointed Girlies in ministry. Thank you for answering the call to the ministry. I know it has not been easy, but I know it will be worth it. You are the apple of God's eye. I need you to stand 10 toes down and spread the good news.

Allow your relationship with God to grow and be purposeful. Allow your experience to be the framework and the anointing to draw new Girlies to Christ. You've suffered for ministry and generational curse-breaking privileges. You answered the call to be a bloodline curse breaker. Do not allow anyone to have power over your judgment.

You are wise enough to differentiate right from wrong. Do not mislead other Girlies in ministry into uncompromised entanglements. Use wisdom, knowledge, and understanding as your weapons against the enemy. Ask the Holy Spirit to give you eyesight as an eagle and ears with sharp, keen hearing. Girl code applies **Psalms 139:14** as a badge of honor.

You are not a carbon copy but a designer's original. You are unstoppable, unmovable, and unshakable. Use your voice as a trumpet and declare what thus says the Lord. You have unlimited opportunities to be of influence and affluence. You are birthing the moves of God on the earth. Be free to spread restoration and the agape love of Christ. Shalom.

Why This Book Title

The Making of a Mean Girl in Ministry was Holy Spirit led. It was birthed from many experiences I and other women in ministry have endured. Many individuals are gifted, titled, and of influence but lack good character, morals, ethics, togetherness, and accountability. Let's be honest: some individuals lack perpetual relationships with other women due to childhood traumas and disappointments from their biological mothers and fathers. Instead of seeking healing, therapy, and counseling, individuals are diligently seeking spiritual parents.

It is a void that needs to be addressed. We can no longer allow these issues to roam free in ministry. Too many divine relationships, collaborations, mentorships, and ministry assignments are being sabotaged by unhealed traumas and impure intentions. In this day and era, individuals are seeking a microwave process, which breeds emulation, imitation, and duplication. Individuals are using their access to keep you balled and chained to them.

It is time to set boundaries, restrictions, and expectations so you will not experience heartbreak nor ministry hurt. Though you are called and chosen, this does not give you permission to act as a witch. Stop using your gift of prophecy to manipulate and congregate. God is searching for individuals who are kingdom-minded. The goal is to birth the moves of God such as Hannah did.

Even though she had an enemy named Peninnah, she was still highly favored by her husband and God. Hannah did not give up. She prayed, worshipped, and trusted in God's timing. At the end of the chapter, Hannah birthed the prophet Samuel into the earth. I am here to remind you to stay focused.

Your ministry may be at a halt, but God is working on your behalf. His glory is the game changer. This is a gift just for you, **Esther 2:17**: *"The king loved her more than the others."* Win individuals to Christ by your heart, pure intentions, clean hands, renewed mindsets, good self-esteem, love, accountability, responsibility, confidence, fashion, individuality, and testimony. I decree **Job 22:28** over your life. Use this scriptural tool to come into the light. You are enough.

Questionnaire

1. After reading this book, are you a mean girl or a girlie in ministry?

_____

_____

_____

_____

_____

2. Who are you accountable to that desires God?

_____

_____

_____

_____

_____

3. What are your issues that are holding you back from being a positive pillar in the ministry community?

_____

_____

_____

_____

_____

4. Have you caused discord with anyone in ministry?

_____

_____

_____

_____

_____

5. What steps have you considered to develop improvement to your character?

_____

_____

_____

_____

_____

6. What has God called you too? Is your election sure?

_____

_____

_____

_____

_____

_____

_____

_____

_____

Girl Code:

Read **Matthew 5:43-47**.

Free Game Girl Code Chip:

Do not clap back on social media, pulpit, conferences, or panels.

Decree **Matthew 5:9-12**.

— Apostle Dr. Crystal Pugh

About the Author

Dr. Tracey Hollis is a dynamic author, women's empowerment speaker, and the visionary founder of Pre'Tea Mixies in the City: That Girl Empowerment Honorees Brunch and Network. Born and raised in Boynton Beach, Florida, and now residing in Columbus, Georgia, she is widely recognized for her vibrant spirit, signature berets, and bold MAC Ruby Woo lipstick, emblems of her unapologetic confidence and faith-driven identity. Dr. Hollis is an alumnus of Miles College in Fairfield, AL.

As a trailblazing leader, Dr. Hollis annually honors five extraordinary women who are "dynamically fastened in their niche," celebrating their excellence through her signature Pre'Tea Mixies empowerment experience. Her mission centers on cultivating sisterhood, authenticity, and divine purpose. In addition to her work with women, Dr. Hollis is a devoted youth mentor. Through programs like Crew Empowerment and The Teen Cave, she hosts monthly gatherings that create safe, empowering spaces for young people to grow spiritually, mentally, and emotionally.

With a message born from personal experience and led by the Holy Spirit, Dr. Hollis is redefining what it means to be "that girl", a kind, confident, and purpose-driven woman of faith. Her movement is not about being a "mean girl in ministry," but a "good girl's girl", a woman committed to uplifting others as she boldly walks in her God-given calling.